The Sanctified Life

Ellen G. White

The Sanctified Life

Copyright © 2019 Indo-European Publishing

The present edition is a reproduction of previous publication of this classic work. Minor typographical errors may have been corrected without note, however, for an authentic reading experience the spelling, punctuation, and capitalization have been retained from the original text.

ISBN: 978-1-64439-121-1

Contents

True and False Theories Contrasted

The sanctification set forth in the Sacred Scriptures has to do with the entire being—spirit, soul, and body. Here is the true idea of entire consecration. Paul prays that the church at Thessalonica may enjoy this great blessing. "The very God of peace sanctify you wholly; and I pray God your whole spirit and soul and body be preserved blameless unto the coming of our Lord Jesus Christ" (1 Thessalonians 5:23).

There is in the religious world a theory of sanctification which is false in itself and dangerous in its influence. In many cases those who profess sanctification do not possess the genuine article. Their sanctification consists in talk and will worship. Those who are really seeking to perfect Christian character will never indulge the thought that they are sinless. Their lives may be irreproachable, they may be living representatives of the truth which they have accepted; but the more they discipline their minds to dwell upon the character of Christ, and the nearer they approach to His divine image, the more clearly will they discern its spotless perfection, and the more deeply will they feel their own defects.

When persons claim that they are sanctified, they give sufficient evidence that they are far from being holy. They fail to see their own weakness and destitution. They look upon themselves as reflecting the image of Christ, because they have no true knowledge of Him. The greater the distance between them and their Saviour, the more righteous they appear in their own eyes.

While with penitence and humble trust we meditate upon Jesus, whom our sins have pierced and our sorrows have burdened, we may learn to walk in His footsteps. By beholding Him we become changed into His divine likeness. And when this work is wrought in us, we shall claim no righteousness of our own, but shall exalt Jesus Christ, while we hang our helpless souls upon His merits.

Self-righteousness Condemned

Our Saviour ever condemned self-righteousness. He taught His disciples that the highest type of religion is that which manifests itself in a quiet, unobtrusive manner. He cautioned them to perform their deeds of charity quietly; not for display, not to be praised or honoured of men, but for the glory of God, expecting their reward hereafter. If they should perform good deeds to be lauded by men, no reward would be given them by their Father in heaven.

The followers of Christ were instructed not to pray for the purpose of being heard of men. "But thou, when thou prayest, enter into thy closet, and when thou hast shut thy door, pray to thy Father which is in secret; and thy Father which seeth in secret shall reward thee openly" (Matthew 6:6). Such expressions as this from the lips of Christ show that He did not regard with approval that kind of piety so prevalent among the Pharisees. His teachings upon the mount show that deeds of benevolence assume a noble form and acts of religious worship shed a most precious fragrance when performed in an unpretending manner, in penitence and humility. The pure motive sanctifies the act.

True sanctification is an entire conformity to the will of God. Rebellious thoughts and feelings are overcome, and the voice of Jesus awakens a new life, which pervades the entire being. Those who are truly sanctified will not set up their own opinion as a standard of right and wrong. They are not bigoted or self-righteousness; but they are jealous of self, ever fearing lest, a promise being left them, they should come short of complying with the conditions upon which the promises are based.

Substituting Feeling for Reason

Many who profess sanctification are entirely ignorant of the work of grace upon the heart. When proved and tested, they are found to be like the self-righteous Pharisee. They will bear no contradiction. They lay aside reason and judgement, and depend wholly upon their feelings, basing their claims to sanctification upon emotions which they have at some time experienced. They are stubborn and perverse in urging their tenacious claims of

2

holiness, giving many words, but bearing no precious fruit as proof. These professedly sanctified persons are not only deluding their own souls by their pretensions, but are exerting an influence to lead astray many who earnestly desire to conform to the will of God. They may be heard to reiterate again and again, "God leads me! God teaches me! I am living without sin!" Many who come in contact with this spirit encounter a dark, mysterious something which they cannot comprehend. But it is that which is altogether unlike Christ, the only true pattern.

Bible sanctification does not consist in strong emotion. Here is where many are led into error. They make feelings their criterion. When they feel elated or happy, they claim that they are sanctified. Happy feelings or the absence of joy is no evidence that a person is or is not sanctified. There is no such thing as instantaneous sanctification. True sanctification is a daily work, continuing as long as life shall last. Those who are battling with daily temptations, overcoming their own sinful tendencies, and seeking for holiness of heart and life, make no boastful claims of holiness. They are hungering and thirsting for righteousness. Sin appears to them exceedingly sinful.

There are those claiming sanctification who make a profession of the truth, like their brethren, and it may be difficult to make a distinction between them; but the difference exists, nevertheless. The testimony of those claiming such an exalted experience will cause the sweet Spirit of Christ to withdraw from a meeting, and will leave a chilling influence upon those present, while if they were truly living without sin, their very presence would bring holy angels into the assembly, and their words would indeed be "like apples of gold in pictures of silver" (Proverbs 25:11).

The Testing Time

In summer, as we look upon the trees of the distant forest, all clothed with a beautiful mantle of green, we may not be able to distinguish between the evergreens and the other trees. But as winter approaches, and the frost king encloses them in his icy embrace, stripping the other trees of their beautiful foliage, the evergreens are readily discerned. Thus it will be with all who are walking in humility, distrustful of self, but clinging tremblingly to the hand of Christ. While those who are self-confident, and trust in their own perfection of character, lose their false robe of righteousness when subjected to the storms of trial, the truly righteous, who sincerely love and fear God, wear the robe of Christ's righteousness in prosperity and adversity alike.

Self-denial, self-sacrifice, benevolence, kindness, love, patience, fortitude, and Christian trust are the daily fruits borne by those who are truly connected with God. Their acts may not be published to the world, but they themselves are daily wrestling with evil, and gaining precious victories over temptation and wrong. Solemn vows are renewed, and kept through the strength gained by earnest prayer and constant watching thereunto. The ardent enthusiast does not discern the struggles of these silent workers; but the eye of Him who seeth the secrets of the heart, notices and regards with approval every effort put forth in lowliness and meekness. It requires the testing time to reveal the pure gold of love and faith in the character. When trials and perplexities come upon the church, then the steadfast zeal and warm affections of Christ's true followers are developed.

We feel sad to see professed Christians led astray by the false and bewitching theory that they are perfect, because it is so difficult to undeceive them and lead them into the right path. They have sought to make the exterior fair and pleasing, while the inward adorning, the meekness and lowliness of Christ, is wanting. The testing time will come to all, when the hopes of many who have for years thought themselves secure, will be seen to be without foundation. When in new positions, under varied circumstances, some who have seemed to be pillars in the house of God reveal only rotten timber beneath the paint and varnish. But the humble in heart, who have daily felt the importance of riveting their souls to the eternal Rock, will stand unmoved amid the tempests of trial, because they trusted not to themselves. "The foundation of God standeth sure, having this seal, The Lord knoweth them that are his" (2 Timothy 2:19).

Normal Fruit Bearing

Those who take pains to call attention to their good works, constantly talking of their sinless state and endeavouring to make their religious attainments prominent, are only deceiving their own souls by so doing. A healthy man, who is able to attend to the vocations of life and who goes forth day after day to his labour with buoyant spirits and with a healthy current of blood flowing through his veins, does not call the attention of every one he meets to his soundness of body. Health and vigour are the natural conditions of his life, and therefore he is scarcely conscious that he is in the enjoyment of so rich a boon.

Thus it is with the truly righteous man. He is unconscious of his goodness and piety. Religious principle has become the spring of his life and conduct, and it is just as natural for him to bear the fruits of the Spirit as for the fig tree to bear figs or for the rosebush to yield roses. His nature is so thoroughly imbued with love for God and his fellow men that he works the works of Christ with a willing heart.

All who come within the sphere of his influence perceive the beauty and fragrance of his Christian life, while he himself is unconscious of it, for it is in harmony with his habits and inclinations. He prays for divine light, and loves to walk in that light. It is his meat and drink to do the will of his heavenly Father. His life is hid with Christ in God; yet he does not boast of this, nor seem conscious of it. God smiles upon the humble and lowly ones who follow closely in the footsteps of the Master. Angels are attracted to them, and love to linger about their path. They may be passed by as unworthy of notice by those who claim exalted attainments and who delight in making prominent their good works, but heavenly angels bend lovingly over them and are as a wall of fire round about them.

Why Christ Was Rejected

Our Saviour was the light of the world, but the world knew Him not. He was constantly employed in works of mercy, shedding light upon the pathway of all; yet He did not call upon those with whom He mingled to behold His unexampled virtue, His self-denial, self-sacrifice, and benevolence. The Jews did not admire such a life. They considered His religion worthless, because it did not accord with their standard of piety. They decided that Christ was not religious in spirit or character; for their religion consisted in display, in praying publicly, and in doing works of charity for effect. They trumpeted their good deeds, as do those who claim sanctification. They would have all understand that they are without sin. But the whole life of Christ was in direct contrast to this. He sought neither gain nor honour. His wonderful acts of healing were performed in as quiet a manner as possible, although He could not restrain the enthusiasm of those who were the recipients of His great blessings. Humility and meekness characterised His life. And it was because of His lowly walk and unassuming manners, which were in such marked contrast to their own, that the Pharisees would not accept Him.

Meekness a Fruit of the Spirit

The most precious fruit of sanctification is the grace of meekness. When this grace presides in the soul, the disposition is moulded by its influence. There is a continual waiting upon God and a submission of the will to His. The understanding grasps every divine truth, and the will bows to every divine precept, without doubting or murmuring. True meekness softens and subdues the heart and gives the mind a fitness for the engrafted word. It brings the thoughts into obedience to Jesus Christ. It opens the heart to the word of God, as Lydia's was opened. It places us with Mary, as learners at the feet of Jesus. "The meek will he guide in judgement: and the meek will he teach his way" (Psalms 25:9).

The language of the meek is never that of boasting. Like the child Samuel, they pray, "Speak, Lord; for thy servant heareth" (1 Samuel 3:9). When Joshua was placed in the highest position of honour, as commander of Israel, he bade defiance to all the enemies of God. His heart was filled with noble thoughts of his great mission. Yet upon the intimation of a message from Heaven he placed himself in the position of a little child to be directed. "What saith my lord unto his servant?" (Joshua 5:14), was his response. The first words of Paul after Christ was revealed to him were, "Lord, what wilt thou have me to do?" (Acts 9:6).

Meekness in the school of Christ is one of the marked fruits of the Spirit. It is a grace wrought by the Holy Spirit as a sanctifier, and enables its possessor at all times to control a rash and

6

impetuous temper. When the grace of meekness is cherished by those who are naturally sour or hasty in disposition, they will put forth the most earnest efforts to subdue their unhappy temper. Every day they will gain self-control, until that which is unlovely and unlike Jesus is conquered. They become assimilated to the Divine Pattern, until they can obey the inspired injunction, "Be swift to hear, slow to speak, slow to wrath" (James 1:19).

When a man professes to be sanctified, and yet in words and works may be represented by the impure fountain sending forth its bitter waters, we may safely say, That man is deceived. He needs to learn the very alphabet of what constitutes the life of a Christian. Some who profess to be servants of Christ have so long cherished the demon of unkindness that they seem to love the unhallowed element and to take pleasure in speaking words that displease and irritate. These men must be converted before Christ will acknowledge them as His children. Meekness is the inward adorning, which God estimates as of great price. The apostle speaks of this as more excellent and valuable than gold or pearls or costly array. While the outward adorning beautifies only the mortal body, the ornament of meekness adorns the soul and connects finite man with the infinite God. This is the ornament of God's own choice. He who garnished the heavens with the orbs of light has by the same Spirit promised that "he will beautify the meek with salvation" (Psalms 149:4). Angels of heaven will register as best adorned those who put on the Lord Jesus Christ and walk with Him in meekness and lowliness of mind.

There are high attainments for the Christian. He may ever be rising to higher attainments. John had an elevated idea of the privilege of a Christian. He says, "Behold, what manner of love the Father hath bestowed upon us, that we should be called the sons of God" (1 John 3:1). It is not possible for humanity to rise to a higher dignity than is here implied. To man is granted the privilege of becoming an heir of God and a joint heir with Christ. To those who have been thus exalted, are unfolded the unsearchable riches of Christ, which are of a thousandfold more value than the wealth of the world. Thus, through the merits of Jesus Christ, finite man is elevated to fellowship with God and with His dear Son.

Daniel's Temperance Principles

The prophet Daniel was an illustrious character. He was a bright example of what men may become when united with the God of wisdom. A brief account of the life of this holy man of God is left on record for the encouragement of those who should afterward be called to endure trial and temptation.

When the people of Israel, their king, nobles, and priests were carried into captivity, four of their number were selected to serve in the court of the king of Babylon. One of these was Daniel, who early gave promise of the remarkable ability developed in later years. These youth were all of princely birth, and are described as "children in whom was no blemish, but well favoured, and skilful in all wisdom, and cunning in knowledge, and understanding science, and such as had ability in them" (Daniel 1:4). Perceiving the superior talents of these youthful captives, King Nebuchadnezzar determined to prepare them to fill important positions in his kingdom. That they might be fully qualified for their life at court, according to Oriental custom, they were to be taught the language of the Chaldeans, and to be subjected for three years to a thorough course of physical and intellectual discipline.

The youth in this school of training were not only to be admitted to the royal palace, but it was provided that they should eat of the meat and drink of the wine which came from the king's table. In all this the king considered that he was not only bestowing great honour upon them, but securing for them the best physical and mental development that could be attained.

Meeting the Test

Among the viands placed before the king were swine's flesh and other meats which were declared unclean by the law of Moses, and which the Hebrews had been expressly forbidden to eat. Here Daniel was brought to a severe test. Should he adhere to the teachings of his fathers concerning meats and drinks, and offend the king, and probably lose not only his position but his life? or should he disregard the commandment of the Lord, and retain the favour of the king, thus securing great intellectual advantages and the most flattering worldly prospects?

Daniel did not long hesitate. He decided to stand firm in his integrity, let the result be what it might. He "purposed in his heart that he would not defile himself with the portion of the king's meat, nor with the wine which he drank" (Daniel 1:8).

Not Narrow or Bigoted

There are many among professed Christians today who would decide that Daniel was too particular, and would pronounce him narrow and bigoted. They consider the matter of eating and drinking as of too little consequence to require such a decided stand—one involving the probable sacrifice of every earthly advantage. But those who reason thus will find in the day of judgement that they turned from God's express requirements and set up their own opinion as a standard of right and wrong. They will find that what seemed to them unimportant was not so regarded of God. His requirements should be sacredly obeyed. Those who accept and obey one of His precepts because it is convenient to do so, while they reject another because its observance would require a sacrifice, lower the standard of right and by their example lead others to lightly regard the holy law of God. "Thus saith the Lord" is to be our rule in all things.

A Faultless Character

Daniel was subjected to the severest temptations that can assail the youth of today; yet he was true to the religious instruction received in early life. He was surrounded with influences calculated to subvert those who would vacillate between principle and inclination; yet the Word of God presents him as a faultless character. Daniel dared not trust to his own moral power. Prayer was to him a necessity. He made God his strength, and the fear of God was continually before him in all the transactions of his life.

9

Daniel possessed the grace of genuine meekness. He was true, firm, and noble. He sought to live in peace with all, while he was unbending as the lofty cedar wherever principle was involved. In everything that did not come in collision with his allegiance to God, he was respectful and obedient to those who had authority over him; but he had so high a sense of the claims of God that the requirements of earthly rulers were held subordinate. He would not be induced by any selfish consideration to swerve from his duty.

The character of Daniel is presented to the world as a striking example of what God's grace can make of men fallen by nature and corrupted by sin. The record of his noble, self-denying life is an encouragement to our common humanity. From it we may gather strength to nobly resist temptation, and firmly, and in the grace of meekness, stand for the right under the severest trial.

God's Approval Dearer Than Life

Daniel might have found a plausible excuse to depart from his strictly temperate habits; but the approval of God was dearer to him than the favour of the most powerful earthly potentate— dearer even than life itself. Having by his courteous conduct obtained favour with Melzar, the officer in charge of the Hebrew youth, Daniel made a request that they might not eat of the king's meat or drink of his wine. Melzar feared that should he comply with this request, he might incur the displeasure of the king, and thus endanger his own life. Like many at the present day, he thought that an abstemious diet would render these youth pale and sickly in appearance and deficient in muscular strength, while the luxurious food from the king's table would make them ruddy and beautiful and would promote physical and mental activity.

Daniel requested that the matter be decided by a ten days' trial— the Hebrew youth during this brief period being permitted to eat of simple food, while their companions partook of the king's dainties. The request was finally granted, and then Daniel felt assured that he had gained his case. Although but a youth, he had seen the injurious effects of wine and luxurious living upon physical and mental health.

God Vindicates His Servant

At the end of the ten days the result was found to be quite the opposite of Melzar's expectations. Not only in personal appearance, but in physical activity and mental vigour, those who had been temperate in their habits exhibited a marked superiority over their companions who had indulged appetite. As a result of this trial, Daniel and his associates were permitted to continue their simple diet during the whole course of their training for the duties of the kingdom.

The Lord regarded with approval the firmness and self-denial of these Hebrew youth, and His blessing attended them. He "gave them knowledge and skill in all learning and wisdom: and Daniel had understanding in all visions and dreams" (Daniel 1:17). At the expiration of the three years of training, when their ability and acquirements were tested by the king, he "found none like Daniel, Hananiah, Mishael, and Azariah: therefore stood they before the king. And in all matters of wisdom and understanding, that the king enquired of them, he found them ten times better than all the magicians and astrologers that were in all his realm" (verse 20).

Self-control a Condition of Sanctification

The life of Daniel is an inspired illustration of what constitutes a sanctified character. It presents a lesson for all, and especially for the young. A strict compliance with the requirements of God is beneficial to the health of body and mind. In order to reach the highest standard of moral and intellectual attainments, it is necessary to seek wisdom and strength from God and to observe strict temperance in all the habits of life. In the experience of Daniel and his companions we have an instance of the triumph of principle over temptation to indulge the appetite. It shows us that through religious principle young men may triumph over the lusts of the flesh and remain true to God's requirements, even though it cost them a great sacrifice.

11

What if Daniel and his companions had made a compromise with those heathen officers and had yielded to the pressure of the occasion by eating and drinking as was customary with the Babylonians? That single instance of departure from principle would have weakened their sense of right and their abhorrence of wrong. Indulgence of appetite would have involved the sacrifice of physical vigour, clearness of intellect, and spiritual power. One wrong step would probably have led to others, until, their connection with Heaven being severed, they would have been swept away by temptation.

God has said, "Them that honour me I will honour" (1 Samuel 2:30). While Daniel clung to his God with unwavering trust, the Spirit of prophetic power came upon him. While he was instructed of man in the duties of court life, he was taught of God to read the mysteries of future ages and to present to coming generations, through figures and similitudes, the wonderful things that would come to pass in the last days.

Controlling the Appetites and Passions

Abstain from fleshy lusts, which war against the soul," is the language of the apostle Peter (1 Peter 2:11). Many regard this text as a warning against licentiousness only, but it has a broader meaning. It forbids every injurious gratification of appetite or passion. Let none who profess godliness regard with indifference the health of the body, and flatter themselves that intemperance is no sin, and will not affect their spirituality. A close sympathy exists between the physical and the moral nature. Any habit which does not promote health degrades the higher and nobler faculties. Wrong habits of eating and drinking lead to errors in thought and action. Indulgence of appetite strengthens the animal propensities, giving them the ascendancy over the mental and spiritual powers.

It is impossible for any to enjoy the blessing of sanctification while they are selfish and gluttonous. Many groan under a burden of infirmities because of wrong habits of eating and drinking, which do violence to the laws of life and health. They are enfeebling their digestive organs by indulging perverted appetite. The power of the human constitution to resist the abuses put upon it is wonderful, but persistent wrong habits in excessive eating and drinking will enfeeble every function of the body. In the gratification of perverted appetite and passion even professed Christians cripple nature in her work and lessen physical, mental, and moral power. Let these feeble ones consider what they might have been had thy lived temperately and promoted health instead of abusing it.

Not an Impossible Standard

When Paul wrote, "The very God of peace sanctify you wholly" (1 Thessalonians 5:23), he did not exhort his brethren to aim at a standard which it was impossible for them to reach; he did not pray that they might have blessings which it was not the will of God to give. He knew that all who would be fitted to meet Christ in peace must possess a pure and holy character. "Every man that striveth for the mastery is temperate in all things. Now they do it to obtain a corruptible crown; but we an incorruptible. I therefore so run, not as uncertainly; so fight I, not as one that beateth the air: but I keep under my body, and bring it into subjection: lest that by any means, when I have preached to others, I myself should be a castaway" (1 Corinthians 9:25-27). "What? know ye not that your body is the temple of the Holy Ghost which is in you, which ye have of God, and ye are not your own? For ye are brought with a price: therefore glorify God in your body, and in your spirit, which are God's" (1 Corinthians 6:19, 20).

An Unblemished Offering

Again, the apostle writes to the believers, "I beseech you therefore, brethren, by the mercies of God, that ye present your bodies a living sacrifice, holy, acceptable unto God, which is your reasonable service" (Romans 12:1). Specific directions were given to ancient Israel that no defective or diseased animal should be presented as an offering to God. Only the most perfect were to be selected for this purpose. The Lord, though the prophet Malachi, most severely reproved His people for departing from these instructions.

"A son honoureth his father, and a servant his master: if then I be a father, where is mine honour? and if I be a master, where is my fear? saith the Lord of hosts unto you, O priests, that despise my name. And ye say, Wherein have we despised thy name? Ye offer polluted bread upon mine altar; and ye say, Wherein have we polluted thee? In that ye say, The table of the Lord is contemptible. And if ye offer the blind for sacrifice, is it not evil? and if ye offer the lame and sick, is it not evil? offer it now unto thy governor; will he be pleased with thee, or accept thy person? saith the Lord of hosts....Ye brought that which was torn, and the lame, and the sick; thus ye brought an offering: should I accept this of your hand? saith the Lord" (Malachi 1:6-13).

Though addressed to ancient Israel, these words contain a lesson for the people of God today. When the apostle appeals to his brethren to present their bodies "a living sacrifice, holy, acceptable unto God," he sets forth the principles of true

14

sanctification. It is not merely a theory, an emotion, or a form of words, but a living, active principle, entering into the everyday life. It requires that our habits of eating, drinking, and dressing be such as to secure the preservation of physical, mental, and moral health, that we may present to the Lord our bodies, not an offering corrupted by wrong habits, but "a living sacrifice, holy, acceptable unto God."

Stimulants and Narcotics

Peter's admonition to abstain from fleshly lusts is a most direct and forcible warning against the use of all such stimulants and narcotics as tea, coffee, tobacco, alcohol, and morphine. These indulgences may well be classed among the lusts that exert a pernicious influence upon moral character. The earlier these hurtful habits are formed, the more firmly will they hold their victim in slavery to lust, and the more certainly will they lower the standard of spirituality.

Bible teaching will make but a feeble impression upon those whose faculties are benumbed by self-gratification. Thousands will sacrifice not only health and life but their hope of heaven before they will wage war against their own perverted appetites. One lady who for many years claimed to be sanctified, made the statement that if she must give up her pipe or heaven she would say, "Farewell, heaven; I cannot overcome my love for my pipe." This idol had been enshrined in the soul, leaving to Jesus a subordinate place. Yet this woman claimed to be wholly the Lord's!

Lusts That War Against the Soul

Wherever they may be, those who are truly sanctified will elevate the moral standard by preserving correct physical habits, and, like Daniel, presenting to others an example of temperance and self-denial. Every depraved appetite becomes a warring lust. Everything that conflicts with natural law creates a diseased condition of the soul. The indulgence of appetite produces a dyspeptic stomach, a torpid liver, a clouded brain, and thus perverts the temper and spirit of the man. And these enfeebled powers are offered to God, who refused to accept the victims for sacrifice unless they were without a blemish! It is our duty to bring our appetites and our habits of life into conformity to natural law. If the bodies offered upon Christ's altar were examined with the close scrutiny to which the Jewish sacrifices were subjected, who would be accepted?

With what care should Christians regulate their habits, that they may preserve the full vigour of every faculty to give to the service of Christ. If we would be sanctified, in soul, body, and spirit, we must live in conformity to the divine law. The heart cannot preserve consecration to God while the appetites and passions are indulged at the expense of health and life. Those who violate the laws upon which health depends, must suffer the penalty. They have so limited their abilities in every sense that they cannot properly discharge their duties to their fellow men, and they utterly fail to answer the claims of God.

When Lord Palmerston, premier of England, was petitioned by the Scotch clergy to appoint a day of fasting and prayer to avert the cholera, he replied, in effect, "Cleanse and disinfect your streets and houses, promote cleanliness and health among the poor, and see that they are plentifully supplied with good food and raiment, and employ right sanitary measures generally, and you will have no occasion to fast and pray. Nor will the Lord hear your prayers while these, His preventives, remain unheeded."

Says Paul, "Let us cleanse ourselves from all filthiness of the flesh and spirit, perfecting holiness in the fear of God" (2 Corinthians 7:1). He presents for our encouragement the freedom enjoyed by the truly sanctified: "There is therefore now no condemnation to them which are in Christ Jesus, who walk not after the flesh, but after the Spirit" (Romans 8:1). He charges the Galatians, "Walk in the Spirit, and ye shall not fulfil the lust of the flesh" (Galatians 5:16). He names some of the forms of fleshly lust — "idolatry,...drunkenness,...and such like" (verses 20, 21). And after mentioning the fruits of the Spirit, among which is temperance, he adds, "And they that are Christ's have crucified the flesh with the affections and lusts" (verse 24).

Tobacco

James says that the wisdom which is from above is "first pure" (James 3:17). If he had seen his brethren using tobacco, would he not have denounced the practice as "earthly, sensual, devilish" (verse 15)? In this age of Christian light, how often the lips that take the precious name of Christ are defiled by tobacco spittle and the breath is polluted with the stench. Surely, the soul that can enjoy such uncleanness must also be defiled. As I have seen men who claimed to enjoy the blessing of entire sanctification, while they were slaves to tobacco, polluting everything around them, I have thought, How would heaven appear with tobacco users in it? God's word has plainly declared that "there shall in no wise enter into it any thing that defileth" (Revelation 21:27). How, then, can those who indulge this filthy habit hope to find admittance there?

Men professing godliness offer their bodies upon Satan's altar and burn the incense of tobacco to his satanic majesty. Does this statement seem severe? Certainly, the offering is presented to some deity. As God is pure and holy, and will accept nothing defiling in its character, He must refuse this expensive, filthy, and unholy sacrifice; therefore we conclude that Satan is the one who claims the honour. Jesus died to rescue man from the grasp of Satan. He came to set us free by the blood of His atoning sacrifice. The man who has become the property of Jesus Christ, and whose body is the temple of the Holy Ghost, will not be enslaved by the pernicious habit of tobacco using. His powers belong to Christ, who has bought him with the price of blood. His property is the Lord's. How, then, can he be guiltless in expending every day the Lord's entrusted capital to gratify an appetite which has no foundation in nature?

An enormous sum is yearly squandered for this indulgence, while souls are perishing for the word of life. Professed Christians rob God in tithes and offerings, while they offer on the altar of destroying lust, in the use of tobacco, more than they give to relieve the poor or to supply the wants of God's cause. Those who are truly sanctified will overcome every hurtful lust. Then all these channels of needless expense will be turned to the Lord's treasury, and Christians will take the lead in self-denial, in self-sacrifice, and in temperance. Then they will be the light of the world.

Tea and Coffee

Tea and coffee, as well as tobacco, have an injurious effect upon the system. Tea is intoxicating. Though less in degree, its effect is the same in character as that of spirituous liquors. Coffee has a greater tendency to becloud the intellect and benumb the energies. It is not so powerful as tobacco, but is similar in its effect. The arguments brought against tobacco may also be urged against the use of tea and coffee.

When those who are in the habit of using tea, coffee, tobacco, opium, or spirituous liquors are deprived of the accustomed indulgence, they find it impossible to engage with interest and zeal in the worship of God. Divine grace seems powerless to enliven or spiritualise their prayers or their testimonies. These professed Christians should consider the source of their enjoyment. Is it from above, or from beneath?

To a user of stimulants, everything seems insipid without the darling indulgence. This deadens the natural sensibilities of both body and mind and renders him less susceptible to the influence of the Holy Spirit. In the absence of the usual stimulant he has a hungering of body and soul, not for righteousness, not for holiness, not for God's presence, but for his cherished idol. In the indulgence of hurtful lusts, professed Christians are daily enfeebling their powers, making it impossible to glorify God.

The Fiery Furnace

In the same year that Daniel and his companions entered the service of the king of Babylon events occurred that severely tested the integrity of these youthful Hebrews and proved before an idolatrous nation the power and faithfulness of the God of Israel.

While King Nebuchadnezzar was looking forward with anxious forebodings to the future, he had a remarkable dream, by which he was greatly troubled, "and his sleep brake from him" (Daniel 2:1). But although this vision of the night made a deep impression on his mind, he found it impossible to recall the particulars. He applied to his astrologers and magicians, and with promises of great wealth and honour commanded them to tell him his dream and its interpretation. But they said, "Tell thy servants the dream, and we will shew the interpretation" (verse 4).

The king knew that if they could really tell the interpretation, they could tell the dream as well. The Lord had in His providence given Nebuchadnezzar this dream, and had caused the particulars to be forgotten, while the fearful impression was left upon his mind, in order to expose the pretensions of the wise men of Babylon. The monarch was very angry, and threatened that they should all be slain if, in a given time, the dream was not made known. Daniel and his companions were to perish with the false prophets; but, taking his life in his hand, Daniel ventures to enter the presence of the king, begging that time may be granted that he may show the dream and the interpretation.

To this request the monarch accedes; and now Daniel gathers his three companions, and together they take the matter before God, seeking for wisdom from the Source of light and knowledge. Although they were in the king's court, surrounded with temptation, they did not forget their responsibility to God. They were strong in the consciousness that His providence had placed them where they were; that they were doing His work, meeting the demands of truth and duty. They had confidence toward God.

19

They had turned to Him for strength when in perplexity and danger, and He had been to them an ever-present help.

The Secret Revealed

The servants of God did not plead with Him in vain. They had honoured Him, and in the hour of trial He honoured them. The secret was revealed to Daniel, and he hastened to request an interview with the king.

The Jewish captive stands before the monarch of the most powerful empire the sun has ever shone upon. The king is in great distress amid all his riches and glory, but the youthful exile is peaceful and happy in his God. Now, if ever, is the time for Daniel to exalt himself, to make prominent his own goodness and superior wisdom. But his first effort is to disclaim all honour for himself and to exalt God as the source of wisdom:

"The secret which the king hath demanded cannot the wise men, the astrologers, the magicians, the soothsayers, shew unto the king; but there is a God in heaven that revealeth secrets, and maketh known to the king Nebuchadnezzar what shall be in the latter days" (Daniel 2:27, 28). The king listens with solemn attention as every particular of the dream is reproduced; and when the interpretation is faithfully given, he feels that he can rely upon it as a divine revelation.

The solemn truths conveyed in this vision of the night made a deep impression on the sovereign's mind, and in humility and awe he fell down and worshiped, saying, "Of a truth it is, that your God is a God of gods, and a Lord of kings, and a revealer of secrets" (verse 47).

The Golden Image

Light direct from Heaven had been permitted to shine upon King Nebuchadnezzar, and for a little time he was influenced by the fear of God. But a few years of prosperity filled his heart with pride, and he forgot his acknowledgement of the living God. He resumed his idol worship with increased zeal and bigotry.

From the treasures obtained in war he made a golden image to represent the one that he had seen in his dream, setting it up in the plain of Dura, and commanding all the rulers and the people to worship it, on pain of death. This statue was about ninety feet in height and nine in breadth, and in the eyes of that idolatrous people it presented a most imposing and majestic appearance. A proclamation was issued calling upon all the officers of the kingdom to assemble at the dedication of the image, and at the sound of the musical instruments, to bow down and worship it. Should any fail to do this, they were immediately to be cast into the midst of a burning fiery furnace.

The appointed day has come, and the vast company is assembled, when word is brought to the king that the three Hebrews whom he has set over the province of Babylon have refused to worship the image. These are Daniel's three companions, who had been called by the king, Shadrach, Meshach, and Abednego. Full of rage, the monarch calls them before him, and pointing to the angry furnace, tells them the punishment that will be theirs if they refuse obedience to his will.

In vain were the king's threats. He could not turn these noble men from their allegiance to the great Ruler of nations. They had learned from the history of their fathers that disobedience to God is dishonour, disaster, and ruin; that the fear of the Lord is not only the beginning of wisdom but the foundation of all true prosperity. They look with calmness upon the fiery furnace and the idolatrous throng. They have trusted in God, and He will not fail them now. Their answer is respectful, but decided: "Be it known unto thee, O king, that we will not serve thy gods, nor worship the golden image which thou hast set up" (Daniel 3:18).

The proud monarch is surrounded by his great men, the officers of the government, and the army that has conquered nations; and all unite in applauding him as having the wisdom and power of the gods. In the midst of this imposing display stand the three youthful Hebrews, steadily persisting in their refusal to obey the king's decree. They had been obedient to the laws of Babylon so far as these did not conflict with the claims of God, but they would not be swayed a hair's breadth from the duty they owed to their Creator.

The king's wrath knew no limits. In the very height of his power and glory, to be thus defied by the representatives of a despised and captive race was an insult which his proud spirit could not endure. The fiery furnace had been heated seven times more than it was wont, and into it were cast the Hebrew exiles. So furious were the flames, that the men who cast them in were burned to death.

In the Presence of the Infinite

Suddenly the countenance of the king paled with terror. His eyes were fixed upon the glowing flames, and turning to his lords, he said, "Did not we cast three men bound into the midst of the fire?" (verse 24). The answer was, "True, O king." And now the monarch exclaimed, "Lo, I see four men loose, walking in the midst of the fire, and they have no hurt; and the form of the fourth is like the Son of God" (verse 25).

When Christ manifests Himself to the children of men, an unseen power speaks to their souls. They feel themselves to be in the presence of the Infinite One. Before His majesty, kings and nobles tremble, and acknowledge that the living God is above every earthly power. With feelings of remorse and shame, the king exclaimed, "Ye servants of the most high God, come forth" (verse 26). And they obeyed, showing themselves unhurt before that vast multitude, not even the smell of fire being upon their garments. This miracle produced a striking change in the minds of the people. The great golden image, set up with such display, was forgotten. The king published a decree that any one speaking against the God of these men should be put to death, "because there is no other God that can deliver after this sort" (verse 29).

Steadfast Integrity and the Sanctified Life

These three Hebrews possessed genuine sanctification. True Christian principle will not stop to weigh consequences. It does not ask, What will people think of me if I do this? or, How will it affect my worldly prospects if I do that? With the most intense longing the children of God desire to know what He would have them do, that their works may glorify Him. The Lord has made ample provision that the hearts and lives of all His followers may be controlled by divine grace, that they may be as burning and shining lights in the world.

These faithful Hebrews possessed great natural ability, they had enjoyed the highest intellectual culture, and now occupied a position of honour; but all this did not lead them to forget God. Their powers were yielded to the sanctifying influence of divine grace. By their steadfast integrity they showed forth the praises of Him who had called them out of darkness into His marvellous light. In their wonderful deliverance were displayed, before that vast assembly, the power and majesty of God. Jesus placed Himself by their side in the fiery furnace, and by the glory of His presence convinced the proud king of Babylon that it could be no other than the Son of God. The light of Heaven had been shining forth from Daniel and his companions, until all their associates understood the faith which ennobled their lives and beautified their characters. By the deliverance of His faithful servants, the Lord declares that He will take His stand with the oppressed and overthrow all earthly powers that would trample upon the authority of the God of heaven.

A Lesson to the Fainthearted

What a lesson is here given to the fainthearted, the vacillating, the cowardly in the cause of God! What encouragement to those who will not be turned aside from duty by threats or peril! These faithful, steadfast characters exemplify sanctification, while they have no thought of claiming the high honour. The amount of good which may be accomplished by comparatively obscure but devoted Christians cannot be estimated until the life records shall be made known, when the judgement shall sit and the books be opened.

Christ identifies His interest with this class; He is not ashamed to call them brethren. There should be hundreds where there is now one among us, so closely allied to God, their lives in such close conformity to His will, that they would be bright and shining lights, sanctified wholly, in soul, body, and spirit.

The conflict still goes on between the children of light and the

23

children of darkness. Those who name the name of Christ should shake off the lethargy that enfeebles their efforts, and should meet the momentous responsibilities that devolve upon them. All who do this may expect the power of God to be revealed in them. The Son of God, the world's Redeemer, will be represented in their words and in their works, and God's name will be glorified.......

As in the days of Shadrach, Meshach, and Abednego, so in the closing period of earth's history the Lord will work mightily in behalf of those who stand steadfastly for the right. He who walked with the Hebrew worthies in the fiery furnace will be with His followers wherever they are. His abiding presence will comfort and sustain. In the midst of the time of trouble—trouble such as has not been since there was a nation—His chosen ones will stand unmoved. Satan with all the hosts of evil cannot destroy the weakest of God's saints. Angels that excel in strength will protect them, and in their behalf Jehovah will reveal Himself as a "God of gods," able to save to the uttermost those who have put their trust in Him.— Prophets and Kings, p. 513.

Daniel in the Lions' Den

When Darius took possession of the throne of Babylon, he at once proceeded to reorganise the government. He "set over the kingdom an hundred and twenty princes...; and over these three presidents; of whom Daniel was first" (Daniel 6:1, 2). And "Daniel was preferred above the presidents and princes, because an excellent spirit was in him; and the king thought to set him over the whole realm" (verse 3). The honours bestowed upon Daniel excited the jealousy of the leading men of the kingdom. The presidents and princes sought to find occasion for complaint against him. "But they could find none occasion nor fault; forasmuch as he was faithful, neither was there any error or fault found in him" (verse 4).

What a lesson is here presented for all Christians. The keen eyes of jealousy were fixed upon Daniel day after day; their watchings were sharpened by hatred; yet not a word or act of his life could they make appear wrong. And still he made no claim to sanctification, but he did that which was infinitely better—he lived a life of faithfulness and consecration.

The more blameless the conduct of Daniel, the greater was the hatred excited against him by his enemies. They were filled with madness, because they could find nothing in his moral character or in the discharge of his duties upon which to base a complaint against him. "Then said these men, We shall not find any occasion against this Daniel, except we find it against him concerning the law of his God" (verse 5). Three times a day Daniel prayed to the God of heaven. This was the only accusation that could be brought against him.

A scheme was now devised to accomplish his destruction. His enemies assembled at the palace and besought the king to pass a decree that no person in the whole realm should ask anything of either God or man, except of Darius the king, for the space of thirty days, and that any violation of this edict should be punished by casting the offender into the den of lions. The king knew nothing of the hatred of these men toward Daniel, and did not suspect that the decree would in any way injure him. Through flattery they made the monarch believe it would be greatly to his honour to pass such an edict. With a smile of satanic triumph upon their faces, they come forth from the presence of the king, and rejoice together over the snare which they have laid for the servant of God.

An Example of Boldness and Fidelity

The decree goes forth from the king. Daniel is acquainted with the purpose of his enemies to ruin him. But he does not change his course in a single particular. With calmness he performs his accustomed duties, and at the hour of prayer he goes to his chamber, and with his windows open toward Jerusalem, he offers his petitions to the God of heaven. By his course of action he fearlessly declares that no earthly power has the right to come between him and his God and tell him to whom he should or should not pray. Noble man of principle! he stands before the world today a praiseworthy example of Christian boldness and fidelity. He turns to God with all his heart, although he knows that death is the penalty for his devotion.

His adversaries watch him an entire day. Three times he has repaired to his chamber, and three times the voice of earnest intercession has been heard. The next morning the complaint is made to the king that Daniel, one of the captives of Judah, has set at defiance his decree. When the monarch heard these words, his eyes were at once opened to see the snare that had been set. He was sorely displeased with himself for having passed such a decree, and laboured till the going down of the sun to devise a plan by which Daniel might be delivered. But the prophet's enemies had anticipated this, and they came before the king with these words: "Know, O king, that the law of the Medes and Persians is, That no decree nor statute which the king establisheth may be changed.

"Then the king commanded, and they brought Daniel, and cast him into the den of lions. Now the king spake and said unto Daniel, Thy God whom thou servest continually, he will deliver thee" (verses 15, 16). A stone was laid upon the mouth of the den, and sealed with the royal seal. "Then the king went to his palace, and passed the night fasting: neither were instruments of musick brought before him: and his sleep went from him" (verse 18).

"My God Hath Sent His Angel"

Early in the morning the monarch hastened to the den of lions, and cried, "Daniel, Oh Daniel, servant of the living God, is thy God, whom thou servest continually, able to deliver thee from the lions?" (verse 20). The voice of the prophet was heard in reply, "Oh king, live for ever. My God hath sent his angel, and hath shut the lions' mouths, that they have not hurt me: forasmuch as before him innocency was found in me; and also before thee, Oh king, have I done no hurt.

"Then was the king exceeding glad for him, and commanded that they should take Daniel up out of the den. So Daniel was taken up out of the den, and no manner of hurt was found upon him, because he believed in his God" (verses 22, 23). Thus was the servant of God delivered. And the snare which his enemies had laid for his destruction proved to be their own ruin. At the command of the king they were cast into the den, and instantly devoured by the wild beasts.

Daniel's Prayers

As the time approached for the close of the seventy years' captivity, Daniel's mind became greatly exercised upon the prophecies of Jeremiah. He saw that the time was at hand when God would give His chosen people another trial; and with fasting, humiliation, and prayer, he importuned the God of heaven in behalf of Israel, in these words: "Oh Lord, the great and dreadful God, keeping the covenant and mercy to them that love him, and to them that keep his commandments; we have sinned, and have committed iniquity, and have done wickedly, and have rebelled, even by departing from thy precepts and from thy judgements; neither have we hearkened unto thy servants the prophets, which spake in thy name to our kings, our princes, and our fathers, and to all the people of the land" (Daniel 9:4-6).

Daniel does not proclaim his own fidelity before the Lord. Instead of claiming to be pure and holy, this honoured prophet humbly identifies himself with the really sinful of Israel. The wisdom which God had imparted to him was as far superior to the wisdom of the great men of the world as the light of the sun shining in the heavens at noonday is brighter than the feeblest star. Yet ponder the prayer from the lips of this man so highly favoured of Heaven. With deep humiliation, with tears and rending of heart, he pleads for himself and for his people. He lays his soul open before God, confessing his own unworthiness and acknowledging the Lord's greatness and majesty.

Earnestness and Fervour

What earnestness and fervour characterise his supplications! The hand of faith is reached upward to grasp the never-failing promises of the Most High. His soul is wrestling in agony. And he has the evidence that his prayer is heard. He knows that victory is his. If we as a people would pray as Daniel prayed, and wrestle as he wrestled, humbling our souls before God, we should realise as marked answers to our petitions as were granted to Daniel. Hear how he presses his case at the court of heaven:

"Oh my God, incline thine ear, and hear; open thine eyes, and behold our desolations, and$the city which is called by thy name; for we do not present our supplications before thee for our righteousnesses, but for thy great mercies. Oh Lord, hear; Oh Lord, forgive; Oh Lord, hearken and do; defer not; for thine own sake, Oh my God: for thy city and thy people are called by thy name" (verses 18, 19). The man of God was praying for the blessing of Heaven upon his people and for a clearer knowledge of the divine will. The burden of his heart was for Israel, who were not, in the strictest sense, keeping the law of God. He acknowledges that all their misfortunes have come upon them in consequence of their transgressions of that holy law. He says, "We have sinned, we have done wickedly....Because for our sins, and for the iniquities of our fathers, Jerusalem and thy people are become a reproach to all that are about us" (verses 15, 16). The Jews had lost their peculiar, holy character as God's chosen people. "Now therefore, O our God, hear the prayer of thy servant, and his supplications, and cause thy face to shine upon thy sanctuary that is desolate" (verse 17). Daniel's heart turns with intense longing to the desolate sanctuary of God. He knows that its prosperity can be restored only as Israel shall repent of their transgressions of God's law, and become humble, faithful, and obedient.

The Heavenly Messenger

As Daniel's prayer is going forth, the angel Gabriel comes sweeping down from the heavenly courts to tell him that his petitions are heard and answered. This mighty angel has been commissioned to give him skill and understanding—to open before him the mysteries of future ages. Thus, while earnestly seeking to know and understand the truth, Daniel was brought into communion with Heaven's delegated messenger. In answer to his petition, Daniel received not only the light and truth which he and his people most needed, but a view of the great events of the future, even to the advent of the world's Redeemer. Those who claim to be sanctified, while they have no desire to search the Scriptures or to wrestle with God in prayer for a clearer understanding of Bible truth, know not what true sanctification is. Daniel talked with God. Heaven was opened before him. But the high honours granted him were the result of humiliation and

29

earnest seeking. All who believe with the heart the word of God will hunger and thirst for a knowledge of His will. God is the author of truth. He enlightens the darkened understanding and gives to the human mind power to grasp and comprehend the truths which He has revealed.

Seeking Wisdom From God

Upon the occasion just described, the angel Gabriel imparted to Daniel all the instruction which he was then able to receive. A few years afterward, however, the prophet desired to learn more of subjects not yet fully explained, and again set himself to seek light and wisdom from God. "In those days I Daniel was mourning three full weeks. I ate no pleasant bread, neither came flesh nor wine in my mouth, neither did I anoint myself at all....Then I lifted up mine eyes, and looked, and behold a certain man clothed in linen, whose loins were girded with fine gold of Uphaz. His body also was like the beryl, and his face as the appearance of lightning, and his eyes as lamps of fire, and his arms and his feet like in colour to polished brass, and the voice of his words like the voice of a multitude" (Daniel 10:2-6).

This description is similar to that given by John when Christ was revealed to him upon the Isle of Patmos. No less a personage than the Son of God appeared to Daniel. Our Lord comes with another heavenly messenger to teach Daniel what would take place in the latter days.

The great truths revealed by the world's Redeemer are for those who search for truth as for hid treasures. Daniel was an aged man. His life had been passed amid the fascinations of a heathen court, his mind cumbered with the affairs of a great empire. Yet he turns aside from all these to afflict his soul before God, and seek a knowledge of the purposes of the Most High. And in response to his supplications, light from the heavenly courts was communicated for those who should live in the latter days. With what earnestness, then, should we seek God, that He may open our understanding to comprehend the truths brought to us from heaven.

"I Daniel alone saw the vision: for the men that were with me

30

saw not the vision; but a great quaking fell upon them, so that they fled to hide themselves....And there remained no strength in me: for my comeliness was turned in me into corruption, and I retained no strength" (verses 7, 8). All who are truly sanctified will have a similar experience. The clearer their views of the greatness, glory, and perfection of Christ, the more vividly will they see their own weakness and imperfection. They will have no disposition to claim a sinless character; that which has appeared right and comely in themselves will, in contrast with Christ's purity and glory, appear only as unworthy and corruptible. It is when men are separated from God, when they have very indistinct views of Christ, that they say, "I am sinless; I am sanctified."

Gabriel now appeared to the prophet, and thus addressed him: "Oh Daniel, a man greatly beloved, understand the words that I speak unto thee, and stand upright: for unto thee am I now sent. And when he had spoken this word unto me, I stood trembling. Then said he unto me, Fear not, Daniel: for from the first day that thou didst set thine heart to understand, and to chasten thyself before thy God, thy words were heard, and I am come for thy words" (verses 11, 12).

Royal Honour to Daniel

What great honour is shown to Daniel by the Majesty of heaven! He comforts His trembling servant and assures him that his prayer has been heard in heaven. In answer to that fervent petition the angel Gabriel was sent to affect the heart of the Persian king. The monarch had resisted the impressions of the Spirit of God during the three weeks while Daniel was fasting and praying, but heaven's Prince, the Archangel, Michael, was sent to turn the heart of the stubborn king to take some decided action to answer the prayer of Daniel.

"And when he had spoken such words unto me, I set my face toward the ground, and I became dumb. And, behold, one like the similitude of the sons of men touched my lips....And said, O man greatly beloved, fear not: peace be unto thee, be strong, yea, be strong. And when he had spoken unto me, I was strengthened, and said, Let my lord speak; for thou hast strengthened me"

31

(verses 15-19). So great was the divine glory revealed to Daniel that he could not endure the sight. Then the messenger of heaven veiled the brightness of his presence and appeared to the prophet as "one like the similitude of the sons of men" (verse 16). By his divine power he strengthened this man of integrity and of faith, to hear the message sent to him from God.

Daniel was a devoted servant of the Most High. His long life was filled up with noble deeds of service for his Master. His purity of character and unwavering fidelity are equalled only by his humility of heart and his contrition before God. We repeat, The life of Daniel is an inspired illustration of true sanctification.

The Character of John

The apostle John was distinguished above his brethren as "the disciple whom Jesus loved." While not in the slightest degree cowardly, weak, or vacillating in character, he possessed an amiable disposition and a warm, loving heart. He seems to have enjoyed, in a pre-eminent sense, the friendship of Christ, and he received many tokens of the Saviour's confidence and love. He was one of the three permitted to witness Christ's glory upon the mount of transfiguration and His agony in Gethsemane; and to the care of John our Lord confided His mother in those last hours of anguish upon the cross.

The Saviour's affection for the beloved disciple was returned with all the strength of ardent devotion. John clung to Christ as the vine clings to the stately pillar. For his Master's sake he braved the dangers of the judgement hall and lingered about the cross; and at the tidings that Christ had risen, he hastened to the sepulchre, in his zeal outstripping even the impetuous Peter.

John's love for his Master was not a mere human friendship, but it was the love of a repentant sinner, who felt that he had been redeemed by the precious blood of Christ. He esteemed it the highest honour to work and suffer in the service of his Lord. His love for Jesus led him to love all for whom Christ died. His religion was of a practical character. He reasoned that love to God would be manifested in love to His children. He was heard again and again to say, "Beloved, if God so loved us, we ought also to love one another" (1 John 4:11). "We love him, because he first loved us. If a man say, I love God, and hateth his brother, he is a liar: for he that loveth not his brother whom he hath seen, how can he love God whom he hath not seen?" (verses 19,20). The apostle's life was in harmony with his teachings. The love which glowed in his heart for Christ, led him to put forth the most earnest, untiring labour for his fellow men, especially for his brethren in the Christian church. He was a powerful preacher, fervent, and deeply in earnest, and his words carried with them a weight of conviction.

A New Creature Through Grace

The confiding love and unselfish devotion manifested in the life and character of John present lessons of untold value to the Christian church. Some may represent him as possessing this love independent of divine grace; but John had, by nature, serious defects of character; he was proud and ambitious, and quick to resent slight and injury.

The depth and fervour of John's affection for his Master was not the cause of Christ's love for him, but the effect of that love. John desired to become like Jesus, and under the transforming influence of the love of Christ, he became meek and lowly of heart. Self was hid in Jesus. He was closely united to the Living Vine, and thus became a partaker of the divine nature. Such will ever be the result of communion with Christ. This is true sanctification.

There may be marked defects in the character of an individual, yet when he becomes a true disciple of Jesus, the power of divine grace makes him a new creature. Christ's love transforms, sanctifies him. But when persons profess to be Christians, and their religion does not make them better men and better women in all the relations of life—living representatives of Christ in disposition and character—they are none of His.

Lessons in Character Building

At one time John engaged in a dispute with several of his brethren as to which of their number should be accounted greatest. They did not intend their words to reach the ear of the Master; but Jesus read their hearts, and embraced the opportunity to give His disciples a lesson of humility. It was not only for the little group who listened to His words, but was to be recorded for the benefit of all His followers to the close of time. "And he sat down, and called the twelve, and saith unto them, If any man desire to be first, the same shall be last of all, and servant of all" (Mark 9:35).

Those who possess the spirit of Christ will have no ambition to occupy a position above their brethren. It is those who are small

34

in their own eyes who will be accounted great in the sight of God. "And he took a child, and set him in the midst of them: and when he had taken him in his arms, he said unto them, Whosoever shall receive one of such children in my name, receiveth me: and whosoever shall receive me, receiveth not me, but him that sent me" (verses 36, 37).

What a precious lesson is this for all the followers of Christ! Those who overlook the life duties lying directly in their pathway, who neglect mercy and kindness, courtesy and love, to even a little child, are neglecting Christ. John felt the force of this lesson and profited by it.

On another occasion his brother James and himself had seen a man casting out devils in the name of Jesus, and because he did not immediately connect himself with their company, they decided that he had no right to do this work, and consequently forbade him. In the sincerity of his heart John related the circumstance to his Master. Jesus said, "Forbid him not: for there is no man which shall do a miracle in my name, that can lightly speak evil of me. For he that is not against us is on our part" (verses 39, 40).

Again, James and John presented by their mother a petition requesting that they might be permitted to occupy the highest positions of honour in Christ's kingdom. The Saviour answered, "Ye know not what ye ask" (Mark 10:38). How little do many of us understand the true import of our prayers! Jesus knew the infinite sacrifice at which that glory must be purchased, when He, "for the joy that was set before him endured the cross, despising the shame" (Hebrews 12:2). That joy was to see souls saved by His humiliation, His agony, and the shedding of His blood.

This was the glory which Christ was to receive, and which these two disciples had requested that they might be permitted to share. Jesus asked them, "Can ye drink of the cup that I drink of? and be baptised with the baptism that I am baptised with? And they said unto him, We can" (Mark 10:38, 39).

How little did they comprehend what that baptism signified! "Jesus said unto them, Ye shall indeed drink of the cup that I drink of; and with the baptism that I am baptised withal shall ye be baptised: but to sit on my right hand and on my left hand is not mine to give; but it shall be given to them for whom it is prepared" (verses 39, 40).

Pride and Ambition Reproved

Jesus understood the motives which prompted the request, and thus reproved the pride and ambition of the two disciples: "Ye know that they which are accounted to rule over the Gentiles exercise lordship over them; and their great ones exercise authority upon them. But so shall it not be among you: but whosoever will be great among you, shall be your minister: and whosoever of you will be the chiefest, shall be servant of all. For even the Son of man came not to be ministered unto, but to minister, and to give his life a ransom for many" (verses 42-45).

Upon one occasion Christ sent messengers before Him unto a village of the Samaritans, requesting the people to prepare refreshments for Himself and His disciples. But when the Saviour approached the town, He appeared to be passing on toward Jerusalem. This aroused the enmity of the Samaritans, and instead of sending messengers to invite and even urge Him to tarry with them, they withheld the courtesies which they would have given to a common wayfarer. Jesus never urges His presence upon any, and the Samaritans lost the blessing which would have been granted them had they solicited Him to be their guest.

We may wonder at this uncourteous treatment of the Majesty of heaven, but how frequently are we who profess to be the followers of Christ guilty of similar neglect. Do we urge Jesus to take up His abode in our hearts and in our homes? He is full of love, of grace, of blessing, and stands ready to bestow these gifts upon us; but, like the Samaritans, we are often content without them.

The disciples were aware of the purpose of Christ to bless the Samaritans with His presence; and when they saw the coldness, jealousy, and disrespect shown to their Master, they were filled with surprise and indignation. James and John were especially stirred. That He whom they so highly reverenced should be thus treated, seemed to them a crime too great to be passed over without immediate punishment. In their zeal they said, "Lord, wilt thou that we command fire to come down from heaven, and consume them, even as Elias did?" (Luke 9:54), referring to the destruction of the Syrian captains and their companies sent out to take the prophet Elijah.

Jesus rebuked His disciples, saying, "Ye know not what manner of spirit ye are of. For the Son of man is not come to destroy men's lives, but to save them" (verses 55, 56). John and his fellow disciples were in a school in which Christ was teacher. Those who were ready to see their own defects, and were anxious to improve in character, had ample opportunity. John treasured every lesson and constantly sought to bring his life into harmony with the Divine Pattern. The lessons of Jesus, setting forth meekness, humility, and love as essential to growth in grace, and a fitness for his work, were of the highest value to John. These lessons are addressed to us as individuals and as brethren in the church, as well as to the first disciples of Christ.

John and Judas

An instructive lesson may be drawn from the striking contrast between the character of John and that of Judas. John was a living illustration of sanctification. On the other hand, Judas possessed a form of godliness, while his character was more satanic than divine. He professed to be a disciple of Christ, but in words and in works denied Him.

Judas had the same precious opportunities as had John to study and to imitate the Pattern. He listened to the lessons of Christ, and his character might have been transformed by divine grace. But while John was earnestly warring against his own faults and seeking to assimilate to Christ, Judas was violating his conscience, 60 yielding to temptation, and fastening upon himself habits of dishonesty that would transform him into the image of Satan.

These two disciples represent the Christian world. All profess to be Christ's followers; but while one class walk in humility and meekness, learning of Jesus, the other show that they are not doers of the word, but hearers only. One class are sanctified through the truth; the other know nothing of the transforming power of divine grace. The former are daily dying to self, and are overcoming sin. The latter are indulging their own lusts, and becoming the servants of Satan.

The Ministry of John

The apostle John passed his early life in the society of the uncultivated fishermen of Galilee. He did not enjoy the training of the schools; but by association with Christ, the Great Teacher, he obtained the highest education which mortal man can receive. He drank eagerly at the fountain of wisdom, and then sought to lead others to that "well of water springing up into everlasting life" (John 4:14). The simplicity of his words, the sublime power of the truths he uttered, and the spiritual fervour that characterised his teachings gave him access to all classes. Yet even believers were unable to fully comprehend the sacred mysteries of divine truth unfolded in his discourses. He seemed to be constantly imbued with the Holy Spirit. He sought to bring the thoughts of the people up to grasp the unseen. The wisdom with which he spoke, caused his words to drop as the dew, softening and subduing the soul.

After the ascension of Christ, John stands forth a faithful, ardent labourer for the Master. With others he enjoyed the outpouring of the Spirit on the day of Pentecost, and with fresh zeal and power he continued to speak to the people the words of life. He was threatened with imprisonment and death, but he would not be intimidated.

Multitudes of all classes come out to listen to the preaching of the apostles, and are healed of their diseases through the name of Jesus, that name so hated among the Jews. The priests and rulers are frantic in their opposition as they see that the sick are healed and Jesus is exalted as the Prince of life. They fear that soon the whole world will believe on Him, and then accuse them of murdering the Mighty Healer. But the greater their efforts to stop this excitement, the more believe on Him and turn from the teachings of the scribes and Pharisees. They are filled with indignation, and laying hands on Peter and John, thrust them into the common prison. But the angel of the Lord, by night, opens the prison doors, brings them forth, and says, "Go, stand and speak in the temple to the people all the words of this life" (Acts 5:20).

With fidelity and earnestness John bore testimony for his Lord upon every suitable occasion. He saw that the times were full of peril for the church. Satanic delusions were existing everywhere. The minds of the people were wandering through the mazes of scepticism and deceptive doctrines. Some who pretended to be true to the cause of God were deceivers. They denied Christ and His gospel and were bringing in damnable heresies and living in transgression of the divine law.

John's Favourite Theme

John's favourite theme was the infinite love of Christ. He believed in God as a child believes in a kind and tender father. He understood the character and work of Jesus; and when he saw his Jewish brethren groping their way without a ray of the Sun of Righteousness to illuminate their path, he longed to present to them Christ, the Light of the world.

The faithful apostle saw that their blindness, their pride, superstition, and ignorance of the Scriptures were riveting upon their souls fetters which would never be broken. The prejudice and hatred against Christ which they obstinately cherished, was bringing ruin upon them as a nation and destroying their hopes of everlasting life. But John continued to present Christ to them as the only way of salvation. The evidence that Jesus of Nazareth was the Messiah was so clear that John declares no man needs to walk in the darkness of error while such light is proffered him.

Saddened by Poisonous Errors

John lived to see the gospel of Christ preached far and near, and thousands eagerly accepting its teachings. But he was filled with sadness as he perceived poisonous errors creeping into the church. Some who accepted Christ claimed that His love released them from obedience to the law of God. On the other hand, many taught that the letter of the law should be kept, also all the Jewish customs and ceremonies, and that this was sufficient for salvation, without the blood of Christ. They held that Christ was a good man, like the apostles, but denied His divinity. John saw the dangers to which the church would be exposed, should they receive these ideas, and he met them with promptness and decision. 64 He wrote to a most honourable helper in the gospel, a lady of good repute and extensive influence: "Many deceivers are entered into the world, who confess not that Jesus Christ is come in the flesh. This is a deceiver and an antichrist. Look to yourselves, that we lose not those things which we have wrought, but that we receive a full reward. Whosoever transgresseth, and abideth not in the doctrine of Christ, hath not God. He that abideth in the doctrine of Christ, he hath both the Father and the Son. If there come any unto you, and bring not this doctrine, receive him not into your house, neither bid him God speed: for he that biddeth him God speed is partaker of his evil deeds" (2 John 7-11).

John was not to prosecute his work without great hindrances. Satan was not idle. He instigated evil men to cut short the useful life of this man of God, but holy angels protected him from their assaults. John must stand as a faithful witness for Christ. The church in its peril needed his testimony.

By misrepresentation and falsehood the emissaries of Satan had sought to stir up opposition against John and against the doctrine of Christ. In consequence dissensions and heresies were imperilling the church. John met these errors unflinchingly. He hedged up the way of the adversaries of truth. He wrote and exhorted, that the leaders in these heresies should not have the least encouragement. There are at the present day evils similar to those that threatened the prosperity of the early church, and the teachings of the apostle upon these points should be carefully heeded. "You must have charity," is the cry to be heard everywhere, especially from those who profess sanctification. But charity is too pure to cover an unconfessed sin. John's teachings are important for those who are living amid the perils of the last days. He had been intimately associated with Christ, he had listened to His teachings and had witnessed His mighty miracles. He bore a convincing testimony, which made the falsehoods of His enemies of none effect.

No Compromise With Sin

John enjoyed the blessing of true sanctification. But mark, the apostle does not claim to be sinless; he is seeking perfection by walking in the light of God's countenance. He testifies that the man who professes to know God, and yet breaks the divine law, gives the lie to his profession. "He that saith, I know him, and keepeth not his commandments, is a liar, and the truth is not in him" (1 John 2:4). In this age of boasted liberality these words would be branded as bigotry. But the apostle teaches that while we should manifest Christian courtesy, we are authorised to call sin and sinners by their right names—that this is consistent with true charity. While we are to love the souls for whom Christ died, and labour for their salvation, we should not make a compromise with sin. We are not to unite with the rebellious, and call this charity. God requires His people in this age of the world to stand, as did John in his time, unflinchingly for the right, in opposition to soul-destroying errors.

No Sanctification without Obedience

I have met many who claimed to live without sin. But when tested by God's word these persons were found to be open transgressors of His holy law. The clearest evidences of the perpetuity and binding force of the fourth commandment failed to arouse the conscience. They could not deny the claims of God, but ventured to excuse themselves in breaking the Sabbath. They claimed to be sanctified, and to serve God on all days of the week. Many good people, they said, did not keep the Sabbath. If men were sanctified, no condemnation would rest upon them if they did not observe it. God was too merciful to punish them for not keeping the seventh day. They would be counted singular in the community should they observe the Sabbath, and would have no influence in the world. And they must be subject to the powers that be.

A lady in New Hampshire bore her testimony in a public meeting that the grace of God was ruling in her heart and that she was wholly the Lord's. She then expressed her belief that this people were doing much good in arousing sinners to see their danger. She said, "The Sabbath that this people present to us is the only Sabbath of the Bible"; and then stated that her mind had been very much exercised upon the subject. She saw great trials before her, which she must meet if she kept the seventh day. The next day she came to meeting and again bore her testimony, saying she had asked the Lord if she must keep the Sabbath, and He had told her she need not keep it. Her mind was now at rest upon that subject. She then gave a most stirring exhortation for all to come to the perfect love of Jesus, where there was no condemnation to the soul.

This woman did not possess genuine sanctification. It was not God who told her that she could be sanctified while living in disobedience to one of His plain commandments. God's law is sacred, and none can transgress it with impunity. The one who told her that she could continue to break God's law and be sinless was the prince of the powers of darkness—the same who told Eve in Eden, through the serpent, "Ye shall not surely die" (Genesis 3:4). Eve flattered herself that God was too kind to punish her for disobedience of His express commands. The same sophistry is urged by thousands in excuse of their disobedience of the fourth commandment. Those who have the mind of Christ will keep all of God's commandments, irrespective of circumstances. The Majesty of heaven says, "I have kept my Father's commandments" (John 15:10).

Adam and Eve dared to transgress the Lord's requirements, and the terrible result of their sin should be a warning to us not to follow their example of disobedience. Christ prayed for His disciples in these words: "Sanctify them through thy truth: thy word is truth" (John 17:17). There is no genuine sanctification except through obedience to the truth. Those who love God with all the heart will love all His commandments also. The sanctified heart is in harmony with the precepts of God's law; for they are holy, just, and good.

God Has Not Changed

God's character has not changed. He is the same jealous God today as when He gave His law upon Sinai and wrote it with His own finger on the tables of stone. Those who trample upon God's holy law may say, "I am sanctified"; but to be indeed sanctified, and to claim sanctification, are two different things.

The New Testament has not changed the law of God. The

sacredness of the Sabbath of the fourth commandment is as firmly established as the throne of Jehovah. John writes: "Whosoever committeth sin transgresseth also the law: for sin is the transgression of the law. And ye know that he was manifested to take away our sins; and in him is no sin. Whosoever abideth in him sinneth not: whosoever sinneth {transgresseth the law} hath not seen him, neither known him" (1 John 3:4-6). We are authorised to hold in the same estimation as did the beloved disciple those who claim to abide in Christ, to be sanctified, while living in transgression of God's law. He met with just such a class as we have to meet. He said, "Little children, let no man deceive you: he that doeth righteousness is righteous, even as he is righteous. He that committeth sin is of the devil; for the devil sinneth from the beginning" (verses 7, 8). Here the apostle speaks in plain terms, as he deemed the subject demanded.

The epistles of John breathe a spirit of love. But when he comes in contact with that class who break the law of God and yet claim that they are living without sin, he does not hesitate to warn them of their fearful deception. "If we say that we have fellowship with him, and walk in darkness, we lie, and do not the truth: but if we walk in the light, as he is in the light, we have fellowship one with another, and the blood of Jesus Christ His Son cleanseth us from all sin. If we say that we have no sin, we deceive ourselves, and the truth is not in us. If we confess our sins, he is faithful and just to forgive us our sins, and to cleanse us from all unrighteousness. If we say that we have not sinned, we make him a liar, and his word is not in us" (1 John 1:6-10).

John in Exile

The wonderful success which attended the preaching of the gospel by the apostles and their fellow labourers increased the hatred of the enemies of Christ. They made every effort to hinder its progress, and finally succeeded in enlisting the power of the Roman emperor against the Christians. A terrible persecution ensued, in which many of the followers of Christ were put to death. The apostle John was now an aged man, but with great zeal and success he continued to preach the doctrine of Christ. He had a testimony of power, which his adversaries could not controvert, and which greatly encouraged his brethren.

When the faith of the Christians would seem to waver under the fierce opposition they were forced to meet, the apostle would repeat, with great dignity, power, and eloquence, "That which was from the beginning, which we have heard, which we have seen with our eyes, which we have looked upon, and our hands have handled, of the Word of life;...that which we have seen and heard declare we unto you, that ye also may have fellowship with us: and truly our fellowship is with the Father, and with his Son Jesus Christ" (1 John 1:1-3).

The bitterest hatred was kindled against John for his unwavering fidelity to the cause of Christ. He was the last survivor of the disciples who are intimately connected with Jesus, and his enemies decided that his testimony must be silenced. If this could be accomplished, they thought the doctrine of Christ would not spread; and if treated with severity, it might soon die out of the world. John was accordingly summoned to Rome to be tried for his faith. His doctrines were misstated. False witnesses accused him as a seditious person, publicly teaching theories which would subvert the nation.

The apostle presented his faith in a clear and convincing manner, with such simplicity and candour that his words had a powerful effect. His hearers were astonished at his wisdom and eloquence. But the more convincing his testimony, the deeper the hatred of those who opposed the truth. The emperor was filled with rage, and blasphemed the name of God and of Christ. He could not controvert the apostle's reasoning or match the power which attended the utterance of truth, and he determined to silence its faithful advocate.

God's Witness Not Silenced

Here we see how hard the heart may become when obstinately set against the purposes of God. The foes of the church were determined to maintain their pride and power before the people. By the emperor's decree, John was banished to the Isle of Patmos, condemned, as he tells us, "for the word of God, and for the testimony of Jesus Christ" (Revelation 1:9). But the enemies of Christ utterly failed in their purpose to silence His faithful witness. From his place of exile comes the apostle's voice, 72 reaching even to the end of time, proclaiming the most thrilling truths ever presented to mortals.

Patmos, a barren rocky island in the Aegean Sea, had been chosen by the Roman government as a place of banishment for criminals. But to the servant of God this gloomy abode proved to be the gate of heaven. He was shut away from the busy scenes of life and from active labour as an evangelist, but he was not excluded from the presence of God. In his desolate home he could commune with the King of kings and study more closely the manifestations of divine power in the book of nature and the pages of inspiration. He delighted to meditate upon the great work of creation and to adore the power of the Divine Architect. In former years his eyes had been greeted with the sight of wood-covered hills, green valleys, and fruitful plains; and in all the beauties of nature he had delighted to trace the wisdom and skill of the Creator. He was now surrounded with scenes that to many would appear gloomy and uninteresting. But to John it was otherwise. He could read the most important lessons in the wild, desolate rocks, the mysteries of the great deep, and the glories of the firmament. To him all bore the impress of God's power and declared His glory.

The Voice of Nature

The apostle beheld around him the witnesses of the Flood, which deluged the earth because the inhabitants ventured to transgress the law of God. The rocks, thrown up from the great deep and from the earth by the breaking forth of the waters, brought vividly to his mind the terrors of that awful outpouring of God's wrath.

But while all that surrounded him below appeared desolate and barren, the blue heavens that bent above the apostle on lonely Patmos were as bright and beautiful as the skies above his own loved Jerusalem. Let man once look upon the glory of the heavens in the night season and mark the work of God's power in the hosts thereof, and he is taught a lesson of the greatness of the Creator in contrast with his own littleness. If he has cherished pride and self-importance because of wealth, or talents, or personal attractions, let him go out in the beautiful night and look upon the starry heavens, and learn to humble his proud spirit in the presence of the Infinite One.

In the voice of many waters—deep calling unto deep —the prophet heard the voice of the Creator. The sea, lashed to fury by the merciless winds, represented to him the wrath of an offended God. The mighty waves, in their most terrible commotion restrained within the limits appointed by an invisible hand, spoke to John of an infinite power controlling the deep. And in contrast he saw and felt the folly of feeble mortals, but worms of the dust, who glory in their wisdom and strength and set their hearts against the Ruler of the universe, as though God were altogether such a one as themselves. How blind and senseless is human pride! Our hour of God's blessing in the sunshine and rain upon the earth will do more to change the face of nature than man with all his boasted knowledge and persevering efforts can accomplish during a lifetime.

In the surroundings of his island home the exiled prophet read the manifestations of divine power, and in all the works of nature held communion with his God. The most ardent longing of the soul after God, the most fervent prayers, went up to heaven from rocky Patmos. As John looked upon the rocks, he was reminded of Christ, the rock of his strength, in whose shelter he could hide without a fear.

A Sabbathkeeper

The Lord's day mentioned by John was the Sabbath, the day on which Jehovah rested after the great work of creation, and which He blessed and sanctified because He had rested upon it. The Sabbath was as sacredly observed by John upon the Isle of Patmos as when he was among the people, preaching upon that day. By the barren rocks surrounding him, John was reminded of rocky Horeb, and how, when God spoke His law to the people there, He said, "Remember the sabbath day, to keep it holy" (Exodus 20:8).

The Son of God spoke to Moses from the mountain-top. God made the rocks His sanctuary. His temple was the everlasting hills. The Divine Legislator descended upon the rocky mountain to speak His law in the hearing of all the people, that they might be impressed by the grand and awful exhibition of His power and glory, and fear to transgress His commandments. God spoke His law amid thunders and lightnings and the thick cloud upon the top of the mountain, and His voice was as the voice of a trumpet exceeding loud. The law of Jehovah was unchangeable, and the tablets upon which He wrote that law were solid rock, signifying the immutability of His precepts. Rocky Horeb became a sacred place to all who loved and revered the law of God.

Shut in With God

While John was contemplating the scenes of Horeb, the Spirit of Him who sanctified the seventh day came upon him. He contemplated the sin of Adam in transgressing the divine law, and the fearful result of that transgression. The infinite love of God, in giving His Son to redeem a lost race, seemed too great for language to express. As he presents it in his epistle he calls upon the church and the world to behold it. "Behold, what manner of love the Father hath bestowed upon us, that we should be called the sons of God: therefore the world knoweth us not, because it knew him not" (1 John 3:1). It was a mystery to John that God

48

could give His Son to die for rebellious man. And he was lost in amazement that the plan of salvation, devised at such a cost to Heaven, should be refused by those for whom the infinite sacrifice had been made.

John was shut in with God. As he learned more of the divine character through the works of creation, his reverence for God increased. He often asked himself, Why do not men, who are wholly dependent upon God, seek to be at peace with Him by willing obedience? He is infinite in wisdom, and there is no limit to His power. He controls the heavens with their numberless worlds. He preserves in perfect harmony the grandeur and beauty of the things which He has created. Sin is the transgression of God's law, and the penalty of sin is death. There would have been no discord in heaven or in the earth if sin had never entered. Disobedience to God's law has brought all the misery that has existed among His creatures. Why will not men be reconciled to God?

It is no light matter to sin against God, to set the perverse will of man in opposition to the will of his Maker. It is for the best interest of men, even in this world, to obey God's commandments. And it is surely for their eternal interest to submit to God, and be at peace with Him. The beasts of the field obey their Creator's law in the instinct which governs them. He speaks to the proud ocean, "Hitherto shalt thou come, but no further" (Job 38:11); and the waters are prompt to obey His word. The planets are marshalled in perfect order, obeying the laws which God has established. Of all the creatures that God has made upon the earth, man alone is rebellious. Yet he possesses reasoning powers to understand the claims of the divine law and a conscience to feel the guilt of transgression and the peace and joy of obedience. God made him a free moral agent, to obey or disobey. The reward of everlasting life—an eternal weight of glory—is promised to those who do God's will, while the threatenings of His wrath hang over all who defy His law.

The Majesty of God

As John meditated upon the glory of God displayed in His works, he was overwhelmed with the greatness and majesty of the

Creator. Should all the inhabitants of this little world refuse obedience to God, He would not be left without glory. He could sweep every mortal from the face of the earth in a moment, and create a new race to people it and glorify His name. God is not dependent on man for honour. He could marshal the starry hosts of heaven, the millions of worlds above, to raise a song of honour and praise and glory to their Creator. "The heavens shall praise thy wonders, O Lord: thy faithfulness also in the congregation of the saints. For who in the heaven can be compared unto the Lord? who among the sons of the mighty can be likened unto the Lord? God is greatly to be feared in the assembly of the saints, and to be had in reverence of all them that are about him" (Psalms 89:5-7).

A Vision of Christ

John calls to remembrance the wonderful incidents that he has witnessed in the life of Christ. In imagination he again enjoys the precious opportunities with which he was once favoured, and is greatly comforted. Suddenly his meditation is broken in upon; he is addressed in tones distinct and clear. He turns to see from whence the voice proceeds, and, lo! he beholds his Lord, whom he has loved, with whom he has walked and talked, and whose sufferings upon the cross he has witnessed. But how changed is the Saviour's appearance! He is no longer "a man of sorrows, and acquainted with grief" (Isaiah 53:3). He bears no marks of His humiliation. His eyes are like a flame of fire; His feet like fine brass, as it glows in a furnace. The tones of His voice are like the musical sound of many waters. His countenance shines like the sun in its meridian glory. In His hand are seven stars, representing the ministers of the churches. Out of His mouth issues a sharp, two-edged sword, an emblem of the power of His word.

John, who has so loved his Lord, and who has steadfastly adhered to the truth in the face of imprisonment, stripes, and threatened death, cannot endure the excellent glory of Christ's presence, and falls to the earth as one stricken dead. Jesus then lays His hand upon the prostrate form of His servant, saying, "Fear not; I am he that liveth, and was dead; and, behold, I am alive for evermore" (Revelation 1:17, 18). John was strengthened to live in the presence of his glorified Lord, and then were presented before him in holy vision the purposes of God for future ages. The glorious attractions of the heavenly home were made known to him. He was permitted to look upon the throne of God, and to behold the white-robed throng of redeemed ones. He heard the music of heavenly angels, and the songs of triumph from those who had overcome by the blood of the Lamb and the word of their testimony.

John's Humility

To the beloved disciple were granted such exalted privileges as have rarely been vouchsafed to mortals. Yet so closely had he become assimilated to the character of Christ that pride found no place in his heart. His humility did not consist in a mere profession; it was a grace that clothed him as naturally as a garment. He ever sought to conceal his own righteous acts and to avoid everything that would seem to attract attention to himself. In his Gospel, John mentions the disciple whom Jesus loved, but conceals the fact that the one thus honoured was himself. His course was devoid of selfishness. In his daily life he taught and practised charity in the fullest sense. He had a high sense of the love that should exist among natural brothers and Christian brethren. He presents and urges this love as an essential characteristic of the followers of Jesus. Destitute of this, all pretensions to the Christian name are vain.

John was a teacher of practical holiness. He presents unerring rules for the conduct of Christians. They must be pure in heart and correct in manners. In no case should they be satisfied with an empty profession. He declares in unmistakable terms that to be a Christian is to be Christlike.

The life of John was one of earnest effort to conform to the will of God. The apostle followed his Saviour so closely, and had such a sense of the purity and exalted holiness of Christ, that his own character appeared, in contrast, exceedingly defective. And when Jesus in His glorified body appeared to John, one glimpse was enough to cause him to fall down as one dead. Such will ever be the feelings of those who know best their Lord and Master. The more closely they contemplate the life and character of Jesus, the more deeply will they feel their own sinfulness, and the less will they be disposed to claim holiness of heart or to boast of their sanctification.

Christian Character

The character of the Christian is shown by his daily life. Said Christ, "Every good tree bringeth forth good fruit; but a corrupt tree bringeth forth evil fruit" (Matthew 7:17). Our Saviour compares Himself to a vine, of which His followers are the branches. He plainly declares that all who would be His disciples must bring forth fruit; and then He shows how they may become fruitful branches. "Abide in me, and I in you. As the branch cannot bear fruit of itself, except it abide in the vine; no more can ye, except ye abide in me" (John 15:4).

The apostle Paul describes the fruit which the Christian is to bear. He says that it "is in all goodness and righteousness and truth" (Ephesians 5:9). And again, "The fruit of the Spirit is love, joy, peace, longsuffering, gentleness, goodness, faith, meekness, temperance" (Galatians 5:22, 23). These precious graces are but the principles of God's law carried out in the life.

The law of God is the only true standard of moral perfection. That law was practically exemplified in the life of Christ. He says of Himself, "I have kept my Father's commandments" (John 15:10). Nothing short of this obedience will meet the requirements of God's word. "He that saith he abideth in him ought himself also so to walk, even as he walked" (1 John 2:6). We cannot plead that we are unable to do this, for we have the assurance, "My grace is sufficient for thee" (2 Corinthians 12:9). As we look into the divine mirror, the law of God, we see the exceeding sinfulness of sin, and our own lost condition as transgressors. But by repentance and faith we are justified before God, and through divine grace enabled to render obedience to His commandments.

Love for God and Man

Those who have genuine love for God will manifest an earnest desire to know His will and to do it. Says the apostle John, whose epistles treat so fully upon love, "This is the love of God, that we keep his commandments" (1 John 5:3). The child who loves his parents will show that love by willing obedience; but the selfish, ungrateful child seeks to do as little as possible for his parents, while he at the same time desires to enjoy all the privileges granted to the obedient and faithful. The same difference is seen among those who profess to be children of God. Many who know that they are the objects of His love and care, and who desire to receive His blessing, take no delight in doing His will. They regard God's claims upon them as an unpleasant restraint, His commandments as a grievous yoke. But he who is truly seeking for holiness of heart and life delights in the law of God, and mourns only that he falls so far short of meeting its requirements.

We are commanded to love one another as Christ has loved us. He has manifested His love by laying down His life to redeem us. The beloved disciple says that we should be willing to lay down our lives for the brethren. For "every one that loveth him that begat loveth him also that is begotten of him" (verse 1). If we love Christ, we shall love those who resemble Him in life and character. And not only so, but we shall love those who have "no hope," and are "without God in the world" (Ephesians 2:12). It was to save sinners that Christ left His home in heaven and came to earth to suffer and to die. For this He toiled and agonised and prayed, until, heartbroken and deserted by those He came to save, He poured out His life on Calvary.

Imitating the Pattern

Many shrink from such a life as our Saviour lived. They feel that it requires too great a sacrifice to imitate the Pattern, to bring forth fruit in good works, and then patiently endure the pruning of God that they may bring forth more fruit. But when the Christian regards himself as only a humble instrument in the hands of Christ, and endeavours to faithfully perform every duty, relying upon the help which God has promised, then he will wear the yoke of Christ and find it easy; then he will bear burdens for Christ, and pronounce them light. He can look up with courage and with confidence, and say, "I know whom I have believed, and am persuaded that he is able to keep that which I have committed unto him" (2 Timothy 1:12).

If we meet obstacles in our path, and faithfully overcome them; if we encounter opposition and reproach, and in Christ's name gain the victory; if we bear responsibilities and discharge our duties in the spirit of our Master—then, indeed, we gain a precious knowledge of His faithfulness and power. We no longer depend upon the experience of others, for we have the witness in ourselves. Like the Samaritans of old, we can say, "We have heard him ourselves, and know that this is indeed the Christ, the Saviour of the world" (John 4:42).

The more we contemplate the character of Christ, and the more we experience of His saving power, the more keenly shall we realise our own weakness and imperfection, and the more earnestly shall we look to Him as our strength and our Redeemer. We have no power in ourselves to cleanse the soul temple from its defilement; but as we repent of our sins against God, and seek pardon through the merits of Christ, He will impart that faith which works by love and purifies the heart. By faith in Christ and obedience to the law of God we may be sanctified, and thus obtain a fitness for the society of holy angels and the white-robed redeemed ones in the kingdom of glory.

Union With Christ Our Privilege

It is not only the privilege but the duty of every Christian to maintain a close union with Christ and to have a rich experience in the things of God. Then his life will be fruitful in good works. Said Christ, "Herein is my Father glorified, that ye bear much fruit" (John 15:8). When we read the lives of men who have been eminent for their piety we often regard their experiences and attainments as far beyond our reach. But this is not the case. Christ died for all; and we are assured in His word that He is more willing to give His Holy Spirit to them that ask Him than are earthly parents to give good gifts to their children. The prophets and apostles did not perfect Christian character by a miracle. They used the means which God had placed within their reach; and all who will put forth the same effort will secure the same results.

Paul's Prayer for the Church

In his letter to the church at Ephesus, Paul sets before them the "mystery of the gospel" (Ephesians 6:19), the "unsearchable riches of Christ" (Ephesians 3:8), and then assures them of his earnest prayers for their spiritual prosperity: "I bow my knees unto the Father of our Lord Jesus Christ,...that he would grant you, according to the riches of his glory, to be strengthened with might by his Spirit in the inner man; that Christ may dwell in your hearts by faith; that ye, being rooted and grounded in love, may be able to comprehend with all saints what is the breadth, and length, and depth, and height; and to know the love of Christ, which passeth knowledge, that ye might be filled with all the fullness of God" (Ephesians 3:14-19).

He writes to his Corinthian brethren also, "to them that are sanctified in Christ Jesus...: Grace be unto you, and peace, from God our Father, and from the Lord Jesus Christ. I thank my God always on your behalf, for the grace of God which is given you by Jesus Christ; that in every thing ye are enriched by him, in all utterance, and in all knowledge; even as the testimony of Christ was confirmed in you: so that ye come behind in no gift; waiting for the coming of our Lord Jesus Christ" (1 Corinthians 1:2-7). These words are addressed not only to the church at Corinth but to all the people of God to the close of time. Every Christian may enjoy the blessing of sanctification.

The apostle continues in these words: "Now I beseech you, brethren, by the name of our Lord Jesus Christ, that ye all speak the same thing, and that there be no divisions among you; but that ye be perfectly joined together in the same mind, and in the same judgement" (verse 10). Paul would not have appealed to them to do that which was impossible. Unity is the sure result of Christian perfection.

In the Epistle to the Colossians also are set forth the glorious privileges vouchsafed to the children of God. "Since we heard of your faith in Christ Jesus, and of the love which ye have to all the saints,...we also, since the day we heard it, do not cease to pray for you, and to desire that ye might be filled with the knowledge of his will in all wisdom and spiritual understanding; that ye might walk worthy of the Lord unto all pleasing, being fruitful in every good work, and increasing in the knowledge of God; strengthened with all might, according to His glorious power, unto all patience and longsuffering with joyfulness" (Colossians 1:4-11).

The Standard of Holiness

The apostle himself was endeavouring to reach the same standard of holiness which he set before his brethren. He writes to the Philippians: "What things were gain to me, those I counted loss for Christ. Yea doubtless, and I count all things but loss for the excellency of the knowledge of Christ Jesus my Lord:...that I may know him, and the power of his resurrection, and the fellowship of his sufferings, being made conformable unto his death; if by any means I might attain unto the resurrection of the dead. Not as though I had already attained, either were already perfect: but I follow after, if that I may apprehend that for which also I am apprehended of Christ Jesus. Brethren, I count not myself to have apprehended: but this one thing I do, forgetting those things which are behind, and reaching forth unto those things which are before, I press toward the mark for the prize of the high calling of God in Christ Jesus" (Philippians 3:7-14). There is a striking contrast between the boastful, self-righteous claims of those who profess to be without sin, and the modest language of the apostle. Yet it was the purity and faithfulness of his own life that gave such power to his exhortations to his brethren.

The Will of God

Paul did not hesitate to enforce, upon every suitable occasion, the importance of Bible sanctification. He says: "Ye know what commandments we gave you by the Lord Jesus. For this is the will of God, even your sanctification" (1 Thessalonians 4:2, 3). "Wherefore, my beloved, as ye have always obeyed, not as in my presence only, but now much more in my absence, work out your own salvation with fear and trembling. For it is God which worketh in you both to will and to do of His good pleasure. Do all things without murmurings and disputings: that ye may be blameless and harmless, the sons of God, without rebuke, in the midst of a crooked and perverse nation, among whom ye shine as lights in the world" (Philippians 2:12-15).

He bids Titus instruct the church that while they should trust to the merits of Christ for salvation, divine grace, dwelling in their hearts, will lead to the faithful performance of all the duties of life. "Put them in mind to be subject to principalities and powers, to obey magistrates, to be ready to every good work, to speak evil of no man, to be no brawlers, but gentle, shewing all meekness unto all men....This is a faithful saying, and these things I will that thou affirm constantly, that they which have believed in God might be careful to maintain good works. These things are good and profitable unto men" (Titus 3:1-8).

Paul seeks to impress upon our minds the fact that the foundation of all acceptable service to God, as well as the very crown of the Christian graces, is love; and that only in the soul where love reigns will the peace of God abide. "Put on therefore, as the elect of God, holy and beloved, bowels of mercies, kindness, humbleness of mind, meekness, longsuffering; forbearing one another, and forgiving one another, if any man have a quarrel against any: even as Christ forgave you, so also do ye. And above all these things put on charity, which is the bond of perfectness. And let the peace of God rule in your hearts, to the which also ye are called in one body; and be ye thankful. Let the word of Christ dwell in you richly in all wisdom; teaching and admonishing one another in psalms and hymns and spiritual songs, singing with grace in your hearts to the Lord. And whatsoever ye do in word or deed, do all in the name of the Lord Jesus, giving thanks to God and the Father of him" (Colossians 3:12-17).

The Christian's Privilege

Many who are sincerely seeking for holiness of heart and purity of life seem perplexed and discouraged. They are constantly looking to themselves, and lamenting their lack of faith; and because they have no faith, they feel that they cannot claim the blessing of God. These persons mistake feeling for faith. They look above the simplicity of true faith, and thus bring great darkness upon their souls. They should turn the mind from self, to dwell upon the mercy and goodness of God and to recount His promises, and then simply believe that He will fulfil His word. We are not to trust in our faith, but in the promises of God. When we repent of our past transgressions of His law, and resolve to render obedience in the future, we should believe that God for Christ's sake accepts us, and forgives our sins.

Darkness and discouragement will sometimes come upon the soul and threaten to overwhelm us, but we should not cast away our confidence. We must keep the eye fixed on Jesus, feeling or no feeling. We should seek to faithfully perform every known duty, and then calmly rest in the promises of God.

The Life of Faith

At times a deep sense of our unworthiness will send a thrill of terror through the soul, but this is no evidence that God has changed toward us, or we toward God. No effort should be made to rein the mind up to a certain intensity of emotion. We may not feel today the peace and joy which we felt yesterday; but we should by faith grasp the hand of Christ, and trust Him as fully in the darkness as in the light.

Satan may whisper, "You are too great a sinner for Christ to save." While you acknowledge that you are indeed sinful and unworthy, you may meet the tempter with the cry, "By virtue of the atonement, I claim Christ as my Saviour. I trust not to my own merits, but to the precious blood of Jesus, which cleanses me. This moment I hang my helpless soul on Christ." The

59

Christian life must be a life of constant, living faith. An unyielding trust, a firm reliance upon Christ, will bring peace and assurance to the soul.

Resisting Temptation

Be not discouraged because your heart seems hard. Every obstacle, every internal foe, only increases your need of Christ. He came to take away the heart of stone, and give you a heart of flesh. Look to Him for special grace to overcome your peculiar faults. When assailed by temptation, steadfastly resist the evil promptings; say to your soul, "How can I dishonour my Redeemer? I have given myself to Christ; I cannot do the works of Satan." Cry to the dear Saviour for help to sacrifice every idol and to put away every darling sin. Let the eye of faith see Jesus standing before the Father's throne, presenting His wounded hands as He pleads for you. Believe that strength comes to you through your precious Saviour.

Viewing With the Eye of Faith

By faith look upon the crowns laid up for those who shall overcome; listen to the exultant song of the redeemed, Worthy, worthy is the Lamb that was slain and hast redeemed us to God! Endeavour to regard these scenes as real. Stephen, the first Christian martyr, in his terrible conflict with principalities and powers and spiritual wickedness in high places exclaimed, "Behold, I see the heavens opened, and the Son of man standing on the right hand of God" (Acts 7:56). The Saviour of the world was revealed to him as looking down from heaven upon him with the deepest interest, and the glorious light of Christ's countenance shone upon Stephen with such brightness that even his enemies saw his face shine like the face of an angel.

If we would permit our minds to dwell more upon Christ and the heavenly world, we should find a powerful stimulus and support in fighting the battles of the Lord. Pride and love of the world will lose their power as we contemplate the glories of that better land so soon to be our home. Beside the loveliness of Christ, all earthly attractions will seem of little worth.

Let none imagine that without earnest effort on their part they can obtain the assurance of God's love. When the mind has been long permitted to dwell only on earthly things, it is a difficult matter to change the habits of thought. That which the eye sees and the ear hears, too often attracts the attention and absorbs the interest. But if we would enter the city of God, and look upon Jesus and His glory, we must become accustomed to beholding Him with the eye of faith here. The words and the character of Christ should be often the subject of our thoughts and of our conversation, and each day some time should be especially devoted to prayerful meditation upon these sacred themes.

Silencing the Spirit

Sanctification is a daily work. Let none deceive themselves with the belief that God will pardon and bless them while they are trampling upon one of His requirements. The wilful commission of a known sin silences the witnessing voice of the Spirit and separates the soul from God. Whatever may be the ecstasies of religious feeling, Jesus cannot abide in the heart that disregards the divine law. God will honour those only who honour Him.

"His servants ye are to whom ye obey" (Romans 6:16). If we indulge anger, lust, covetousness, hatred, selfishness, or any other sin, we become servants of sin. "No man can serve two masters" (Matthew 6:24). If we serve sin, we cannot serve Christ. The Christian will feel the promptings of sin, for the flesh lusteth against the Spirit; but the Spirit striveth against the flesh, keeping up a constant warfare. Here is where Christ's help is needed. Human weakness becomes united to divine strength, and faith exclaims, "Thanks be to God, which giveth us the victory through our Lord Jesus Christ" (1 Corinthians 15:57)!

Correct Religious Habits

If we would develop a character which God can accept, we must form correct habits in our religious life. Daily prayer is as essential to growth in grace, and even to spiritual life itself, as is temporal food to physical well-being. We should accustom ourselves to lift the thoughts often to God in prayer. If the mind wanders, we must bring it back; by persevering effort, habit will finally make it easy. We cannot for one moment separate ourselves from Christ with safety. We may have His presence to attend us at every step, but only by observing the conditions which He Himself has laid down.

Religion must be made the great business of life. Everything else should be held subordinate to this. All our powers, of soul, body, and spirit, must be engaged in the Christian warfare. We must look to Christ for strength and grace, and we shall gain the victory as surely as Jesus died for us.

The Value of the Soul

We must come nearer to the cross of Christ. Penitence at the foot of the cross is the first lesson of peace we have to learn. The love of Jesus—who can comprehend it? Infinitely more tender and self-denying than a mother's love! If we would know the value of a human soul, we must look in living faith upon the cross, and thus begin the study which shall be the science and the song of the redeemed through all eternity. The value of our time and our talents can be estimated only by the greatness of the ransom paid for our redemption. What ingratitude do we manifest toward God when we rob Him of His own by withholding from Him our affections and our service! Is it too much to give ourselves to Him who has sacrificed all for us? Can we choose the friendship of the world before the immortal honours which Christ proffers— "to sit with me in my throne, even as I also overcame, and am set down with my Father in his throne" (Revelation 3:21)?

A Progressive Work

Sanctification is a progressive work. The successive steps are set before us in the words of Peter: "Giving all diligence, add to your faith virtue; and to virtue knowledge; and to knowledge temperance; and to temperance patience; and to patience godliness; and to godliness brotherly kindness; and to brotherly kindness charity. For if these things be in you, and abound, they make you that ye shall neither be barren nor unfruitful in the knowledge of our Lord Jesus Christ" (2 Peter 1:5-8). "Wherefore the rather, brethren, give diligence to make your calling and election sure: for if ye do these things, ye shall never fall: for so an entrance shall be ministered unto you abundantly into the everlasting kingdom of our Lord and Saviour Jesus Christ" (verses 10, 11).

Here is a course by which we may be assured that we shall never fall. Those who are thus working upon the plan of addition in obtaining the Christian graces have the assurance that God will work upon the plan of multiplication in granting them the gifts of His Spirit. Peter addresses those who obtained like precious faith: "Grace and peace be multiplied unto you through the knowledge of God, and of Jesus our Lord" (verse 2). By divine grace, all who will may climb the shining steps from earth to heaven, and at last, "with songs and everlasting joy" (Isaiah 35:10), enter through the gates into the city of God.

Our Saviour claims all there is of us; He asks our first and holiest thoughts, our purest and most intense affection. If we are indeed partakers of the divine nature, His praise will be continually in our hearts and upon our lips. Our only safety is to surrender our all to Him and to be constantly growing in grace and in the knowledge of the truth.

Paul's Shout of Victory

The apostle Paul was highly honoured of God, being taken in holy vision to the third heaven, where he looked upon scenes whose glories he was not permitted to reveal. Yet this did not lead him to boastfulness or self-confidence. He realised the importance of constant watchfulness and self-denial, and plainly declares, "I keep under my body, and bring it into subjection: lest that by any means, when I have preached to others, I myself should be a castaway" (1 Corinthians 9:27).

Paul suffered for the truth's sake, and yet we hear no complaints from his lips. As he reviews his life of toil and care and sacrifice, he says, "I reckon that the sufferings of this present time are not worthy to be compared with the glory which shall be revealed in us' (Romans 8:18). The shout of victory from God's faithful servant comes down the line to our time: "Who shall separate us from the love of Christ? shall tribulation, or distress, or persecution, or famine, or nakedness, or peril, or sword?...Nay, in all these things we are more than conquerors through him that loved us. For I am persuaded, that neither death, nor life, nor angels, nor principalities, nor powers, nor things present, nor things to come, nor height, nor depth, nor any other creature, shall be able to separate us from the love of God, which is in Christ Jesus our Lord" (Romans 8:35-39).

Though Paul was at last confined in a Roman prison —shut away from the light and air of heaven, cut off from his active labours in the gospel, and momentarily expecting to be condemned to death—yet he did not yield to doubt or despondency. From that gloomy dungeon came his dying testimony, full of a sublime faith and courage that has inspired the hearts of saints and martyrs in all succeeding ages. His words fitly describe the results of that sanctification which we have in these pages endeavoured to set forth: "I am now ready to be offered, and the time of my departure is at hand. I have fought a good fight, I have finished my course, I have kept the faith: henceforth there is laid up for me a crown of righteousness, which the Lord, the righteous judge, shall give me at that day: and not to me only, but unto all them also that love his appearing" (2 Timothy 4:6-8).